The publisher will be pleased to make good any omissions or rectify any mistakes brought to their attention at the earliest opportunity.

Copyright ©2019 by Kevin Black.

All rights reserved. No part of this book may be reproduced in any form on by an electronic or mechanical means, including information storage and retrieval systems, without permission in writing from the publisher, except by a reviewer who may quote brief passages in a review.

Illustrations by Hatice Bayramoglu

Print ISBN: 978-1-7336993-0-3

E-book: 978-1-7336993-1-0

Library of Congress Control Number: 2019901778

Thank you.

A nursery-rhyme book for moms

Dear Mom

by Kevin Black

illustrated by:
Hatice Bayramoglu

I love you!

From the comfort you gave,

To the way you taught me to behave,

You'll always be my mom.

Sometimes they are truly missed.

You should do more

There always nice and warm, like a s'more.

I know your love extends for miles;

Even if our laughs are contagious once in a while

You always just looked at me and smiled.

DON'T GET ME WRONG, I LOVE DAD TOO

But, this gift isn't for him, it's for you.

Tell him, he's coming up in the queue

But for now, it's time to get back to

you.

You always had plenty and kept me snug.

You taught me well

and because of you, I'll always prevail.

Like a guardian angel you never fail.

I think by now that reaction is just

organic,

Ya know, like I'm on the Titanic.

Except, I'm not in the Atlantic.

So, when someone else doesn't, you know I

look at them like they a yeti,

Probably because they're super petty.

Just because my mom is hot and ready.

Just so they can talk about my mom

looking like a glass of fine wine.

Especially since they need to know that our

genes are divine.

So, once again thanks for this

bloodline.

Your cooking is still the real deal.

Hey, sometime let me take that wheel

So, I can cook you up something you'll like;

not just some oatmeal.

But not one of them crusty ones where their meat looks like it came from a horse.

Because mom, you deserve a fiesta,

But that's okay in this modern era.

I know I get my good looks from you,

So, thank you for not making me look like no kangaroo.

Catch you on the flip side,

Bye-bye

THIS IS JUST A RHYME-BOOK TO TELL YOU THAT I LOVE YOU,

And I'm grateful, because of you I got spunk

Like I always said, momma didn't raise any

punk.

Until next time,

I love you and this!

#Winning

To my special lady, here is a pass which is:

Good for

20 minutes of

Mommy Time

I think any mom could use this but you…

you deserve this.

Besides, who even cares if it's 9:00 in the morning?

This page is for you, mom, you can write anything you want. Whether it's how much you love this, a 2-page scrapbook or your to-do list for tomorrow, this page is for **you**:

Continued here, mom!

Of course I can make you food,

while i'm on the toilet

Right Now...

#MommyProblems

Is this just the norm?

A	C	Y	P	E	T	T	Y	O	U	Y
L	U	F	I	T	U	A	E	B	Y	A
R	X	Z	P	M	E	T	F	A	D	E
R	T	B	M	R	U	S	D	S	T	T
B	R	B	L	Q	E	S	E	T	X	S
M	A	V	N	U	R	D	S	P	H	S
G	O	D	D	E	S	S	Q	U	E	E
E	Q	L	H	E	U	I	P	Q	L	R
U	E	T	M	N	L	K	M	O	M	P
B	O	M	Z	G	O	D	V	H	K	M
M	T	L	P	H	V	Y	R	T	X	E
M	A	J	E	T	O	F	U	G	O	D
Q	U	E	X	U	P	Y	M	M	O	M
M	A	H	A	M	A	M	E	S	S	Y

MOMMY POWERS ACTIVATE

Mothers Day Love Extra

Mom Queen Empress

Petty Beautiful Goddess

Mommy You Mama

The *Child & Mommy* Contract

I _____, certify that I am the child of _____. She is the woman who loves me, cares for me & my laziness, and totally does not hold anything that 5 year old me and younger said that may or may not have been true, against me. My promise to you is to always love you forever.

I _____, certify that I am the Mommy, of my lovely child _____.
Therefore, I promise to always protect you and love you unconditionally forever.

C	A	Y	P	E	T	T	P	R	U	P
G	K	E	N	T	U	A	E	B	Y	A
N	N	I	P	N	E	T	F	A	R	E
S	T	O	F	R	F	G	C	S	E	T
L	C	B	R	I	S	S	E	T	H	S
I	A	H	E	T	R	L	S	L	H	A
A	O	R	O	E	S	T	I	C	N	L
Y	C	L	H	C	U	I	U	A	L	O
E	E	T	C	A	O	P	H	O	N	N
L	O	C	I	C	C	L	A	S	G	H
P	T	A	P	A	E	U	A	T	Y	E
R	A	K	K	T	O	U	U	T	A	I
U	U	E	E	U	T	I	A	H	E	H
P	A	I	L	Y	T	U	A	E	B	I
B	E	A	U	T	G	N	O	R	T	C

"You could NEVER have too many crossword puzzles"
- The author's mom

Beauty	Chocolate	Cake
Nails	Salon	Cupcake
Purple	Fierce	Strong

Hearts up, smiles big,

I love you, Mom

This page is dedicated to the inspiration of this book, the author's mom, Stephanie Black.

LOVE YOU MOM,

Kevin Black

www.ingramcontent.com/pod-product-compliance
Lightning Source LLC
Chambersburg PA
CBHW041220070526
44584CB00001B/28